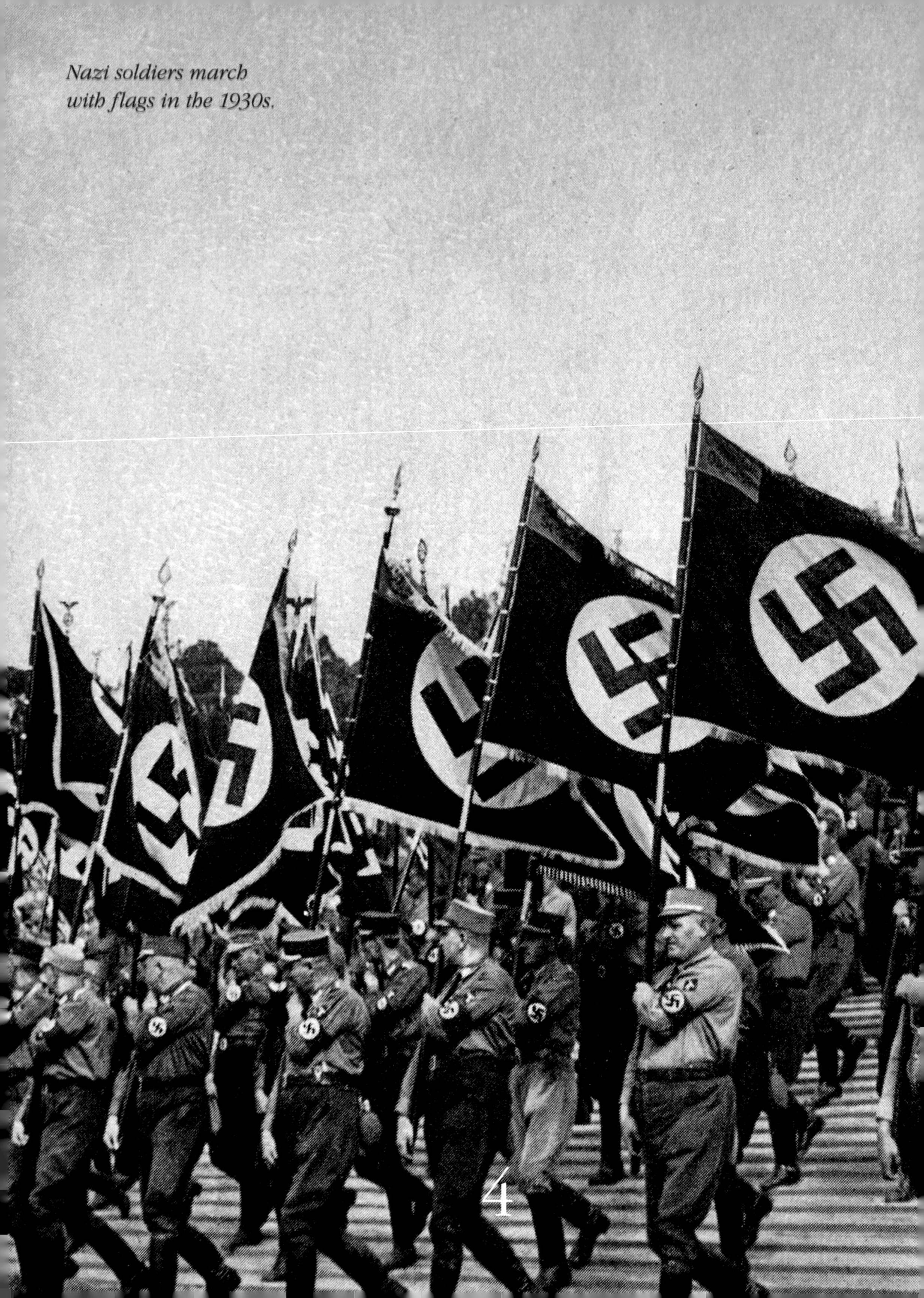

Nazi soldiers march with flags in the 1930s.

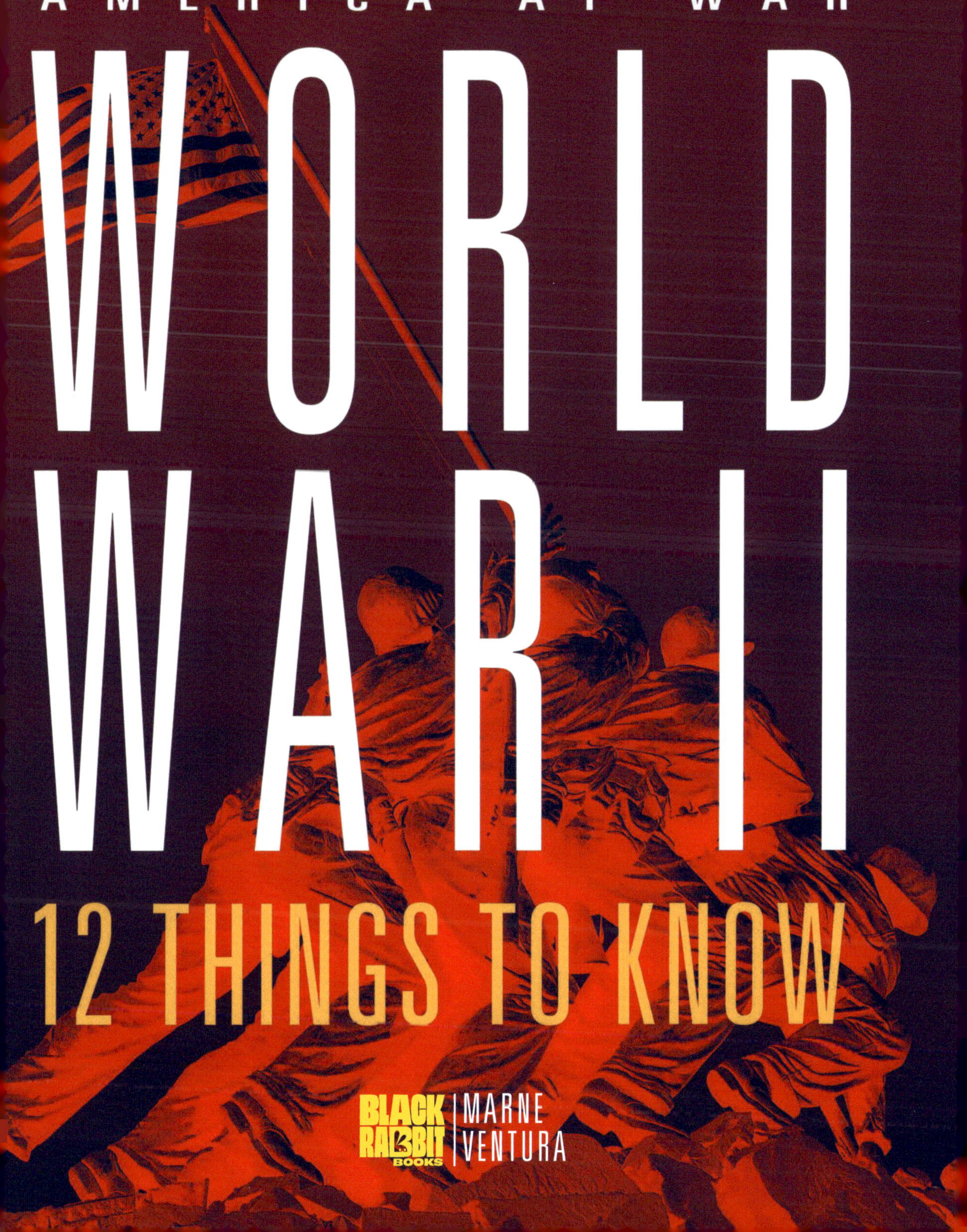

AMERICA AT WAR

WORLD WAR II

12 THINGS TO KNOW

BLACK RABBIT BOOKS | MARNE VENTURA

Table of Contents

Tensions Rise in *Europe*

1

World War I was fought between 1914 and 1918. More than 10 million people had died. Another 21 million had been injured. It was called "the war to end all wars." But it did not end all wars. It left countries in ruins. Their governments were weak. This allowed a new power to rise: **fascism**. Fascist countries were ruled by one person. The leaders were called **dictators**. Italy, Japan, and Germany were led by dictators. They vowed to make their countries strong again. The most powerful leader was Adolf Hitler.

Nazi Party symbol includes a swastika and German eagle.

Hitler became the head of Germany on January 30, 1933. He led the Nazi Party. He built a strong police force. He built up a large army. Hitler wanted more land for Germany. His army began to **invade** other countries. One area was Czechoslovakia. Part of the country was home to many Germans.

Great Britain, France, and Italy signed a deal with Germany in September 1938. It was called the Munich **Pact**. Germany would get the part of Czechoslovakia that he wanted. In return, Hitler would not take over the rest of the country. In March 1939, he went back on his word. His army took Czechoslovakia. Then Hitler attacked Poland. The British government said they would help Poland. They did not want Germany to take more of Europe.

THINK ABOUT IT Find out more about the causes of World War II. Which do you think was the most important? Give reasons for your answer.

Adolf Hitler

British Prime Minister Neville Chamberlain holds an agreement signed by himself and Hitler after the Munich Pact.

3 million Number of Germans in Czechoslovakia in 1938.

Benito Mussolini brought fascism to Italy in the 1920s. • Fascism places the power of the state above human rights. • Its dictators have total power over a country.

Hitler *Invades* Poland

2

Germany attacked Poland on September 1, 1939. The fight is known as the Battle of Westerplatte. Two days later, Great Britain declared war on Germany. France was also allied with Poland. It joined the fight too. World War II had begun.

Hitler did not want a long war. He had a plan called the blitzkrieg. This means "lightning war." Hitler lined up his armies along a thin strip of land. His ground and air forces stormed enemy lines. Then German tanks rushed in. Surprised enemies were easily beaten.

Hitler's forces swept through nine countries in nine months. Denmark and Belgium were the first. Hitler took France in May of 1940. With Italy's help, they also took Greece. By April 1941, Germany had captured much of Europe.

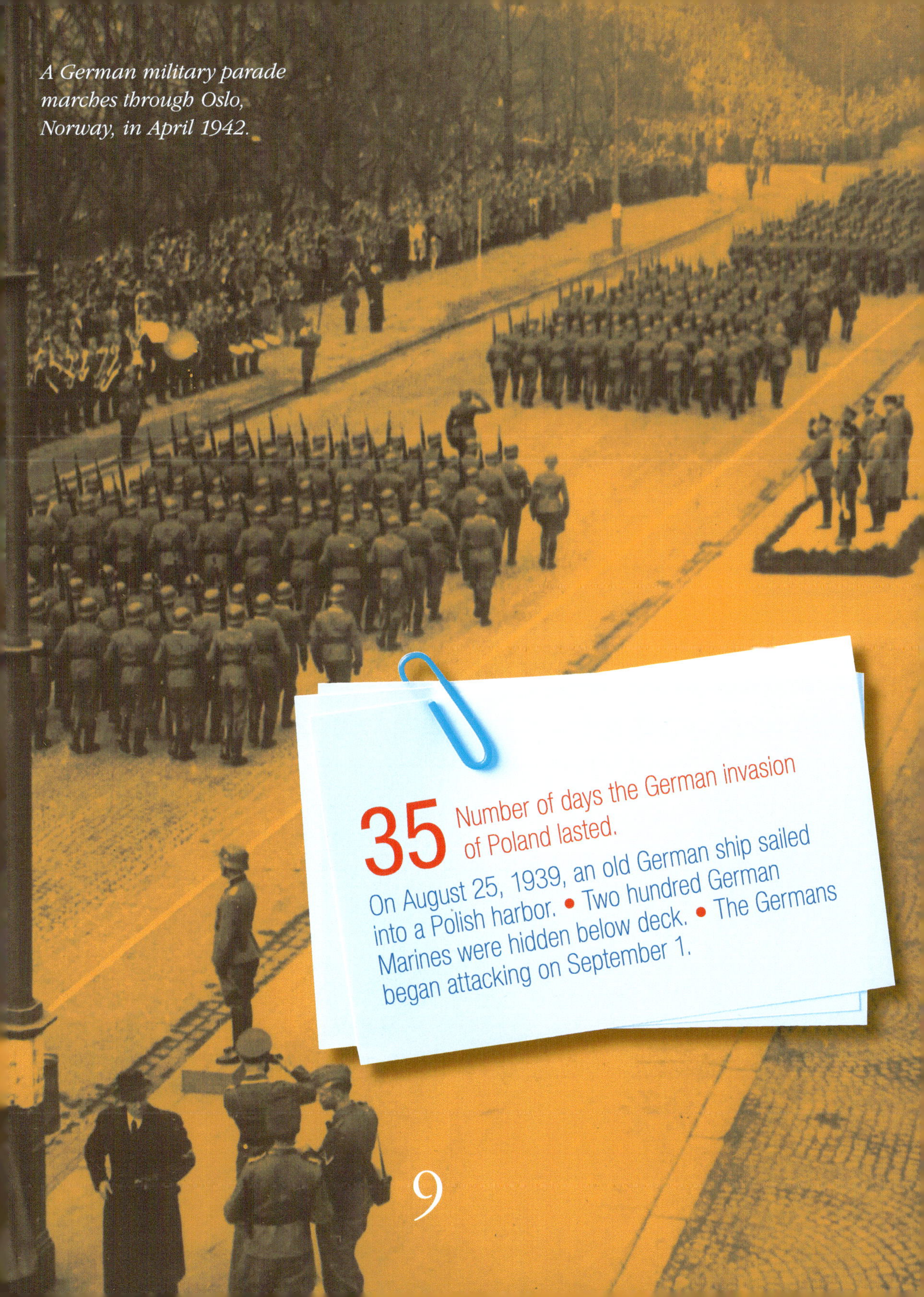

A German military parade marches through Oslo, Norway, in April 1942.

35 Number of days the German invasion of Poland lasted.

On August 25, 1939, an old German ship sailed into a Polish harbor. • Two hundred German Marines were hidden below deck. • The Germans began attacking on September 1.

Hitler was **antisemitic**. He believed white Germans were a superior **race**. Anyone different was lesser. He blamed Jews for Germany's problems. Hitler created a police force called the SS. They arrested anyone Hitler said was guilty of crimes against Germany. This included Jewish, Romani, and Slavic people. They were taken to prison camps.

The Westerplatte Monument honors those who died to protect Poland.

THE PHONY WAR After Hitler invaded Poland, there were declarations of war. But little fighting occurred. There were some sea attacks. But neither side made land attacks. Instead, a British raid dropped leaflets over Germany. They spread the evils of the Nazi Party. This lasted for months. Newspapers called it the Phony War. It lasted until May 1940.

Axis Powers Line Up *for War*

3

Adolf Hitler made two important deals in 1936. The first was with Italy. The other was with Japan. In 1940, the three countries agreed to work together. Italy was led by Benito Mussolini. Japan was led by Emperor Hirohito. Together, they made the Axis Powers

The three countries helped each other. They all wanted to claim new lands. They also wanted to get rid of **communism**. Each of the leaders would keep control of his own land. They would never attack each other. A deal was struck. Germany and Italy would rule

Adolf Hitler

Benito Mussolini

Emperor Hirohito

Europe. Japan would control Asia. The agreement was signed on September 27, 1940. The Axis forces were ready to take Europe by storm.

Other nations joined later. Some did so by choice. Others were forced. Hungary was the first to join the Axis. Romania and Bulgaria joined next. Then Yugoslavia and Croatia. By June 1941, nine countries had signed the deal. They would help each other if one country was attacked. This was meant to prevent the United States from entering the war. So far, the United States had been **neutral**. The Axis hoped it would stay that way.

12 Number of months between the start of World War II and the Axis agreement.

Germany and Italy were already allies. • Italy wanted protection from the Soviet Union. • Japan would fight against the Soviet Union. • The Soviet Union was made of 15 republics including Russia.

A propaganda poster shows the flags of the Allied Powers.

4 Japan Bombs *Pearl Harbor*

US President Franklin D. Roosevelt saw what was happening in Europe. He wanted to help. But most Americans wanted to stay out of the war. The country had lost more than 100,000 men in World War I. They did not want to send more. There were other ways to help, though. Weapons were sent to the Allied Powers. These were countries fighting against Germany.

Everything changed on December 7, 1941. Japanese planes flew over Pearl Harbor, Hawaii, at 7:55 am. There was an American naval base there. It was an important location. From there, ships and planes could move quickly to Japan. If Japan destroyed those forces, there would be nothing to fear.

The Japanese planes bombed the US airfields. They attacked navy ships. Smoke and flames rose from the harbor. Oil burned in the water. Some sailors had to

2,403 Number of Americans killed at Pearl Harbor.

The attack was a surprise. • Japanese ships carried planes 3,500 miles (5,633 kilometers) from Japan to Hawaii. • The ships kept their radios turned off. This kept US **radar** from spotting them.

The bombing sunk several American ships, including the USS Arizona.

dive in. Others were injured from bullet wounds. Some had broken limbs. Many died.

When the bombing ended, many of the ships were sunk or badly damaged. The attack killed thousands. Americans were shocked. They feared Japan would attack the mainland next.

The next day, President Roosevelt gave a speech to Congress. He said December 7 was "a date which will live in infamy." Overnight, opinions had changed. America was ready to enter the fight. The United States declared war on Japan. On December 11, Germany and Italy declared war on the United States. The conflict became a true world war.

Pearl Harbor is now a national memorial in Hawaii.

Allied Powers Prepare to *Fight Back*

5

The United States joined the Allied Powers. They were one of the Big Three. The other two were Great Britain and the Soviet Union. These countries had the biggest military forces. They were the key to victory. President Roosevelt led the United States. Winston Churchill was in charge of Great Britain. Joseph Stalin headed the Soviet Union.

The Allies wanted to restore peace. But they all had different ideas of how to do it. Roosevelt wanted to end fascism. He wanted to spread **democracy** throughout the world. Churchill wanted to crush Germany. He wanted to stop it from rising again. Stalin wanted that too. He also wanted to spread communism.

Statue of President Roosevelt and Winston Churchill

Soviet leader Joseph Stalin

The Big Three worked together. They made battle plans. They worked to free France and other countries under Hitler's control. Winning the war and stopping the Nazis was their end goal.

Other countries joined the Allies. They came from six continents. Canada and Mexico joined from North America. Bolivia and Brazil were a few from South America. Eight other European countries jumped in. China and the Philippines joined from Asia. India, under British control, joined too. South Africa and Ethiopia signed from Africa.

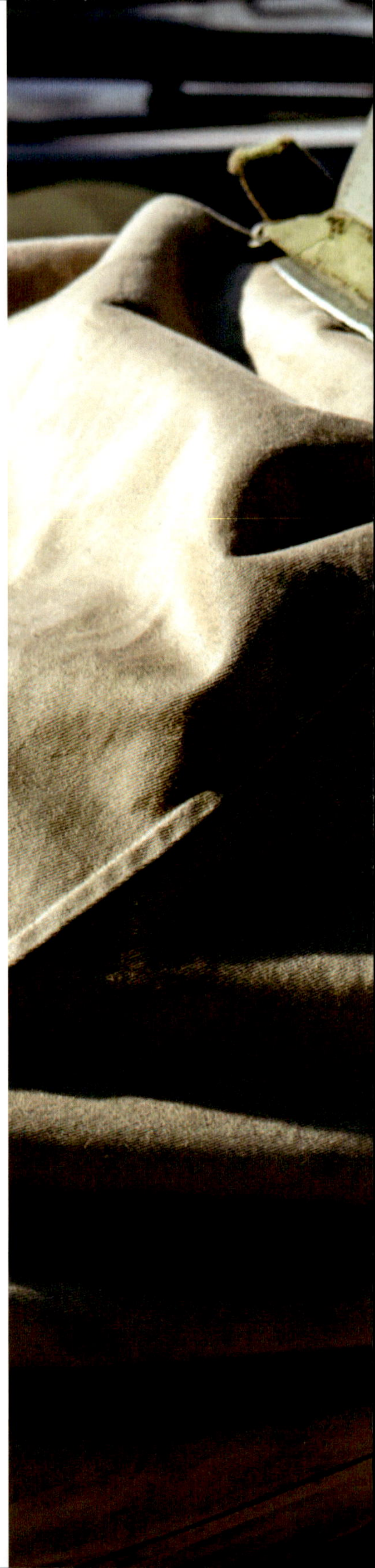

An American soldier takes aim against an enemy.

Posters were used to encourage people to join the army.

US Soldiers Ship Out *Overseas*

6

Despite being neutral, the US military was already planning for war. A **draft** was put into law in 1940. At first, men between the ages of 21 and 45 had to register for service. By 1942, the draft expanded to men ages 18 to 64. The military quickly grew to 10 million. By 1945, 16 million men had served in the war. Most draftees were sent to the army.

The army had many weapons. They had rifles and machine guns for ground fighting. Rocket launchers and tanks could clear enemy troops. Navy aircraft carriers launched planes into the air from flight decks. The planes carried bombs and machine guns. Some had torpedoes and rockets. Army air force pilots flew strike aircraft. They used firepower to fight at close range. The war had two main areas of attack. The biggest spanned across all of Europe. The Allies wanted to defeat Hitler there first. Then the other Axis Powers would fall. The plan was called "Europe First". US troops fought in Italy, the Mediterranean, and North Africa. The Battle of the Atlantic was part of this plan. It was the longest **campaign** in the war. The Atlantic was key for shipping new supplies. US troops also fought in the Pacific. Until 1944, more Americans were sent here than to Europe. They battled the Japanese who controlled much of this region.

US paratroopers prepare to jump.

50 million Number of men registered for the WWII draft.

The new law said men must sign up to fight. • A lottery chose who would serve. • Service lasted for at least one year.

Submarine torpedoes were used to attack unsuspecting ships.

Life Changes for Americans *at Home*

7

Not everyone could fight overseas. But there were many ways Americans could help fight at home. Ration stamps were handed out in the spring of 1942. The stamps were used to buy food and clothing. They limited how much gas could be purchased. Groups held drives for tin cans and rubber tires. These items were made into weapons and bullets.

It was important to keep factories going. They made guns and tanks instead of appliances. With men drafted to fight, the factories lost many workers. Women took their place.

The war was expensive. To help, the government created war **bonds**. This was a type of loan. People bought a bond for $18.75. In 10 years, it could be cashed in for more. From 1941 to 1945, 85 million

6 million Number of women who served in jobs in defense industries.

A famous poster of Rosie the Riveter called for women to help with the war effort. • Women made tanks, ships, and planes. • Women also replaced men in sports, music, and leadership roles.

Americans had bought nearly $186 billion in bonds. That money helped fund the war.

Life changed even more for Japanese Americans. People stopped trusting them. Many feared they might help Japan during the war. In 1942, President Roosevelt signed an executive order. The new law called for nearly 120,000 Japanese Americans to be taken from their homes. They were sent to live in prison camps.

$100 war bond from 1944

THINK ABOUT IT

How would you have helped during the war? Write down three things you could have done.

8

Battle of Midway Rages in *the Pacific*

Pearl Harbor had been a success for Japan. Their next target was Midway Island. There was a US Navy base located there. The island was halfway between the United States and Asia. Planes and ships often stopped there to refuel.

Japan planned to draw out the US fleet. When the ships tried to fight back, Japan would destroy them. Allied agents picked up Japanese messages. By early May 1942, they knew an attack was coming. Soon, they found out when and where it would take place. Three US aircraft carriers waited to surprise the Japanese.

On June 4, Japanese planes attacked Midway. Then they tried to fly back to four aircraft carriers. The Americans were ready to strike. Their bombers attacked the Japanese fleet. The strike went on for two days. All four carriers were destroyed. The Japanese suffered heavy

3,057 Number of Japanese people who died at Midway.

The Japanese lost four carriers and one cruiser. They also lost hundreds of planes. • The US lost 362 men and 144 planes. One carrier and one destroyer went down. • Japan had hoped to make Midway a base to attack Pearl Harbor again.

losses. Finally, the Japanese forces gave up. They returned to Japan.

The victory at Midway was a turning point in the Pacific. Japan's control over the Pacific began to shrink.

US Navy bombers fly on mission in the Pacific.

Battle of Stalingrad Ends in *German Defeat*

9

War was raging at sea and on land. On June 22, 1941, the Germans moved into the Soviet Union. More than 3 million Axis troops were on the ground. They killed or captured 900,000 people.

The Soviets had not been ready for the attack. However, the German soldiers were not ready for winter. The freezing weather was devastating. Germany backed off until spring. This gave both sides time to find more men and weapons.

In September 1942, the German army attacked Stalingrad, Russia. The Germans hoped it would be a fast fight. But the Russians fought back for months. The Germans were running out of men and weapons. The Soviet army circled around them. There would be no giving up, though. Hitler told his men to hold their ground at all costs.

When winter came again, many Germans starved to death. Around 150,000 died. The army was down to 91,000 men. The Battle of Stalingrad was one of the bloodiest in history. On February 2, 1943, the Germans gave up.

The battle was another turning point in the war. The Allies had stopped Germany's push into the Soviet Union. Now, Stalin began to move his troops west. It was time for payback.

The German army attacks at Stalingrad in November 1942.

2 million Number of soldiers who were killed or wounded in the Battle of Stalingrad.

Stalingrad was an important city on the Volga River. • The city was named for the Soviet leader Joseph Stalin. • Hitler's code name for the invasion was Operation Barbarossa.

HOLOCAUST IN GERMANY

Soldiers were not the only target of the war. Jews were rounded up and shot. Hitler built concentration camps around Europe. Jews were shot or poisoned with gas at the camps. Some were forced to work until they died. About 6 million Jews were murdered. Millions of other people lost their lives as well. This was called the Holocaust.

Men recreate the events of 1943 that ended the Battle of Stalingrad.

D-Day Leads to Victory *in Europe*

10

In 1943, Allied forces gathered in Great Britain. Hitler believed they would attack the coast of France. But he did not know its exact location. In November, he ordered his troops to finish building the Atlantic Wall. It ran along the coast of Europe. It was more than 2,400 miles (3,862 km) long. There were trenches and bunkers. Mines dotted the land.

The Allied attack began at dawn on June 6, 1944. Thousands of paratroopers landed behind enemy lines. They took over bridges and roads. Other Allied forces landed on the beaches of Normandy, France. They rode in on 5,000 ships and landing craft. Nearly 11,000 aircraft flew overhead. It was one of the largest raids in history. Men ran through the water and onto the beach. Many lost their lives storming the Atlantic Wall. The invasion was called D-Day.

Land mine equipment

150,000 Number of Allied troops that landed in Normandy, France, on D-Day.

It was the largest land, air, and water invasion in the history of warfare. • The code name for the invasion was Operation Overlord. • "D-Day" is a term for the start date of any military operation.

US paratroopers get ready to board their planes.

The Allies had full control of the beaches in a week. They never looked back. By the end of August, they reached Paris, France. It was the beginning of the end for Hitler. Allied forces moved east toward Germany. Soviet troops moved west. The Nazis were in the middle. There was nowhere to go. Hitler took his life on April 30. On May 7, 1945, Germany surrendered.

Soldiers wade onto the Normandy beach from boats on D-Day in 1944.

PREPARING FOR D-DAY Operation Bodyguard took place before D-Day. Allies set up fake military forces 150 miles (241 km) northeast of Normandy. They used fake aircraft and ships. They had inflatable tanks and dummy paratroopers. The plan was to fool the Germans. They gave them incorrect information about when and where the attack would be.

US Bombing Causes Japan *to Surrender*

11

It was the summer of 1945. Japan's navy and air force were ruined. Bombings left the country in shreds. The Allies planned a final attack. It was set for November. Officials knew that many lives would be lost on both sides. But hopefully, it would end the war.

On July 16, the United States tested a new weapon. It was the world's first **atomic bomb**. The secret test took place in the desert of New Mexico. They called the test Trinity. Some people doubted the bomb would go off at all. Others wondered if the whole world would be torn apart. The bomb was dropped. The test went perfectly.

Bockscar *was the B-29 bomber that dropped the atomic bomb on Nagasaki, Japan.*

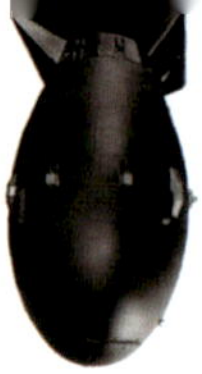

The atomic bombs were called "Fat Man" and "Little Boy."

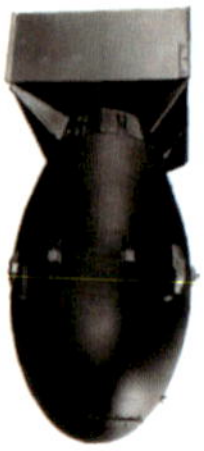

Ten days later, the Allies offered Japan a chance to surrender. If they refused, Japan's military and homeland would be destroyed. Japan did not back down.

The Japanese expected a ground attack. But on August 6, a single US B-29 plane flew over the city of Hiroshima. It dropped an atomic bomb. Tens of thousands of people were killed. Many more died later from wounds, burns, and **radiation**. Still, Japan's leaders did not give up. They wanted Emperor Hirohito to remain in power.

Meanwhile, the Soviet Union attacked Japanese-led Manchuria. More than 1 million Japanese soldiers were killed. On August 9, the United States dropped another atomic bomb. It destroyed Nagasaki, Japan. On August 15, 1945, Hirohito surrendered. World War II was finally over.

80,000 Estimated number of people killed in the bombing of Hiroshima.

About another 70,000 people died later of radiation poisoning. • The program that developed the bombs was called the Manhattan Project. • President Harry Truman wanted to end the war quickly.

Each atomic bomb created a massive mushroom cloud.

THINK ABOUT IT

Historians still debate whether the use of atomic bombs was needed. What do you think?

High Price of War *Takes Its Toll*

12

More than 50 countries fought in World War II. Sixty million people died. Millions more were injured. Many countries lost more than 10 percent of their population. Many people lost their homes and everything they owned. About 6 million European Jews were killed in the Holocaust. It was a terrible **genocide**.

World War II is the most expensive war in history. The total cost was more than $1 trillion. The United States alone spent 10 times more than all its earlier wars put together. Property damage totaled more than $239 billion.

Once world powers, the war left Germany and Japan in ruins. They had no leaders. The Soviet Union emerged as a new superpower. It shared its ideals with new countries. Communism spread throughout Europe and Asia. This would lead to more wars.

2 New superpowers created by World War II.

The United States and Soviet Union became rivals for power and status. • Their military forces were far greater than other countries. • This rivalry would fuel the Cold War from 1947 to 1991.

Victims of the atomic bomb in Nagasaki

America also became a new superpower. Before the war, its military was small during peacetimes. After WWII, the US draft ended. Troop numbers dropped to 684,000 by 1947. But America began to invest more in its military. It created new bases around the world. Soldiers remained in Germany, Italy, Turkey, and Japan. America was ready to defend democracy against any future threats.

Auschwitz was the biggest concentration camp in Poland. The sign says, "Work sets you free."

12 Key Dates

January 30, 1933
Adolf Hitler becomes the chancellor of Germany.

September 1, 1939
German forces invade Poland.

September 3, 1939
Great Britain and France declare war on Germany.

September 16, 1940
US begins to draft men into military service.

December 7, 1941
Japan bombs Pearl Harbor, Hawaii. America declares war on Japan the next day.

June 6, 1942
Americans defeat Japan in Battle of Midway.

September 1, 1939

December 7, 1941

September 16, 1940

February 2, 1943
Germans surrender in the Battle of Stalingrad.

June 6, 1944
Allied forces begin the D-Day invasion in Normandy, France.

April 30, 1945
Hitler commits suicide.

May 7, 1945
Germany surrenders to the Allied forces.

August 6, 1945
A US B-29 bomber drops the first atomic bomb on Hiroshima, Japan.

August 15, 1945
Japan surrenders.

June 6, 1942

June 6, 1944

August 6, 1945

Glossary

antisemitic
Having extreme hatred towards Jewish people.

atomic bomb
A bomb with great explosive power.

bond
An official document in which a government or company promises to pay back an amount of money, plus interest.

campaign
A series of military battles and attacks designed to produce a particular result in a war.

communism
A society in which the government owns the things that are used to make and transport goods and there is not private property.

democracy
A type of government where representatives are elected by the whole population.

dictator
A ruler with total power over a country.

draft
A system that requires people to join the military for a period of time.

fascism
A political movement led by a dictator.

genocide
The planned killing of a large number of people from a particular nation or race.

invade
To enter a place in large numbers.

neutral
Staying out of a conflict.

pact
A formal agreement between two or more parties.

race
A group of people who share the same history, language, and culture.

radar
A system for detecting objects that uses high-frequency electromagnetic waves.

radiation
A dangerous and powerful energy that comes from nuclear reactions.

For More Information

Books

Adamson, Thomas K. *World War II.* Parker, CO: The Child's World, 2024.

Smibert, Angie. *12 Incredible Facts about the D-Day Invasion.* Mankato, MN: Black Rabbit Books, 2025.

Ventura, Marne. *12 Iconic American Battles.* Mankato, MN: Black Rabbit Books, 2025.

Websites

Attack of Pearl Harbor
kids.nationalgeographic.com/history/article/pearl-harbor

World War II
kids.britannica.com/students/article/World-War-II/277798

World War II in Europe
education.nationalgeographic.org/resource/world-war-ii-europe/

About the Author

Marne Ventura is a children's book author and a former elementary school teacher. She holds a master's degree in education with an emphasis in reading and language development from the University of California.

Index

TOP RANK is published by Black Rabbit Books, P.O. Box 227, Mankato, MN, 56002. •

• Designed by Danny Nanos • Photographs © Alamy Stock Photo/Barry Lewis, 23, Ian G Dagnall, 37, 45, Shawshots, 13; Associated Press/Unknown, 21, 22; Dreamstime/Unknown, 10, 18, 20, 44–45; Getty Images/Bettmann, 3, 38, 39, 45, Bettmann, 41; Library of Congress/Unknown, 14; Public Domain/Al_Skiff, 35; Shutterstock/adolf martinez soler, 5, Alexyz3d, 39, Andreas Wolochow, 4–5, 8, Belinda Pretorius, 48, Charlesimage, 11, Everett Collection, 15, 44, 2, 28–29, 45, 30–31, 35, 36, 45, 37, 41, G_D Photography, 42–43, GizmoPhoto, 27, 28, Images from Jeffrey, 34, J. Helgason, 23, Jim Lambert, 34, JohnatAPW, 34, Jolygon, 46–47, jorik, cover, 1, Krysek, 18-19, Matt Gibson, 17, meunierd, 11, MikhailSh, 32–33, murathakanart, 6, Olga Popova, 11, Penny Hicks, 17, S D Walsh, 16, TSViPhoto, 40, Zvonimir Atletic, 11; Wikimedia Commons/J. Howard Miller, 24, 25, JHerbstman, 26, National Digital Archives, 7, 9, 44

Library of Congress Cataloging-in-Publication Data: Names: Ventura, Marne, author. | Title: World War II: 12 things to know / by Marne Ventura. | Other titles: World War II, twelve things to know | Description: Mankato, MN: Top Rank, an imprint of Black Rabbit Books, 2026. | Series: America at war | Includes bibliographical references and index. | Ages 9–13 | Grades 4–6 | Identifiers: LCCN 2024050093 | ISBN 9781644668276 (library binding) | ISBN 9781644668597 (paperback) | ISBN 9781644668917 (ebook) | Subjects: LCSH: World War, 1939-1945—Juvenile literature. | Classification: LCC D743.7 .V468 2026 | DDC 940.54—dc23/eng/20241206 | LC record available at https://lccn.loc.gov/2024050093